DOUGLAS HAIG

Defeat Into Victory

Gordon Corrigan

First published by Endeavour Press Ltd in 2015.

This edition published by Sharpe Books in 2018.

Table of Contents

Introduction

Apart perhaps from Oliver Cromwell, no figure in British military history is the subject of such violently opposing views as Field Marshal Sir Douglas Haig. But while Cromwell was loathed or loved in his lifetime, the hatred of Haig began after his death; and while eighty-seven years after Cromwell's death he had been largely forgotten, Haig's name even today arouses powerful emotions. In 1998 the *Daily Express* mounted a campaign to remove Haig's statue from Whitehall, on the grounds that he was an incompetent butcher of a million British soldiers. That we actually lost less than three quarters of a million and that they were not all in the army, and were not all lost on the Western Front, and that Haig was not in command on the Western Front for the first year of the war, and that it was actually the Germans who killed all those British soldiers and sailors seems to have passed the tabloid journals by. Nevertheless, the depth of feeling against Haig is enormous and has somehow come to be linked with the 2006 decision by politicians to pardon those executed for military offences between 1914 and 1918. The popular view of Haig today is that he was unfit to command Britain's armies on the Western Front, that he obtained his promotion through his social and royal connections, that he was obsessed with horsed cavalry, that he was a technophobe incapable of appreciating the advantages of mechanisation, that he was out of touch with what was happening at the front, that he was incapable of planning anything but headlong frontal attacks against machine guns and barbed wire, and that he was indifferent to the suffering of his men. All those deaths on the Western Front were unnecessary and were the direct result of Haig's uncaring incompetence.

Vituperation directed against Haig and the generals started when it became apparent that the government could not produce a 'land fit for heroes' after the war, and people looked for someone to blame. Basil Liddell Hart, and other men like him, started to express military opinions which excused his own behaviour in the Great War, where he had lacked, at least in his own estimation, if not that of others, the one quality esteemed by soldiers above all others – bravery under fire. As a belief in collective security and the universal brotherhood of man – a false belief as it turned out – took hold in the nineteen-thirties, so people began to question the way the war had been conducted, and the politicians, anxious not to be blamed themselves, pushed the blame on to the generals who couldn't hit back. All this was aided and abetted by the so-called war poets, and after a brief interlude for the Second World War – immeasurably more incompetently conducted than the First – criticism of the First World War generals started again, peaking with the play and film 'Oh What a Lovely War', and the TV series 'Blackadder Goes Forth'.

Historical events are proved or disproved by the evidence of reliable witnesses, and with the release under the various disclosure rules of most files relating to the Great War, it is now much easier to investigate the evidence relating to Haig than it once was. In this book I seek to examine the career of Douglas Haig and see if we can separate truth from legend. What are the criticisms of Haig? Does the evidence support those criticisms, and if not, why do people believe them?

We have to remember that Haig was the last of his kind, in that he was not only the operational commander but the supreme commander too. He had to direct the British part of the war on the Western Front but he also had to answer directly to the British Government and to colonial and Dominion governments in relation to their contingents. He had to liaise directly with the military allies and also deal with the French and Belgian governments in regard to the two and a half million men plonked down in their territory with all the legal, administrative and cultural problems thus created. That never happened again nor would it happen now. In the Second World War Montgomery always had an Alexander or an Eisenhower flying top cover for him, somebody to take the burden of political communication, and much of the administration and personnel matters, away from him, leaving him to get on with commanding the troops. Haig did not have that luxury and his position was far more akin to that of Marlborough or Wellington than it was to Montgomery or Slim.

When examining any aspect of British participation in the First World War we have to bear in mind three basic facts: firstly, this was a coalition war and Britain was the junior partner on land. It was not up to British politicians or British generals to decide what to do; rather they had to accept that he who paid the piper – the French with their vastly bigger army covering far more of the Front – called the tune. Secondly, this war was unique in that it was the only war, before or since, when virtually the whole of the British Army was fighting the main enemy, the Germans, in the main theatre, the Western Front, for the whole of the war. Thirdly, despite what some historians alleged and still allege, this was a necessary war. Britain could not have stayed aloof: she had a moral and practical obligation to Belgium, which was, after all, a British creation, and the launch of seventeen modern battleships between 1908 and 1914 by Germany, when she had neither an empire to defend nor trade routes to protect, could only have had one purpose: to take on the Royal Navy at some stage. Had Britain not entered the War then France would have lost and the United Kingdom would have been the next victim, in a war that she could not necessarily have been won.

If we look at the war through Anglo-centric eyes some of the British operations make little sense – the Somme and Passchendaele spring to mind – but if we zoom out and look at the war as a whole, the logic begins to appear. We cannot properly understand the Somme unless we know what was happening at Verdun 120 miles to the south and Passchendaele makes little sense unless one is aware of the state of the French army in 1917 where there were wholesale mutinies.

We also need to bear in mind that it is no use trying to play basketball under the rules of rugby. Similarly it is pointless to impose the standards of today on the society of a century ago. Then, the technology to fight short, sharp, economic campaigns – helicopters, smart bombs, armoured personal carriers, satellite intelligence, did not exist. The death penalty was regarded as a perfectly normal sanction, both under military law and in the civilian world. While Britain was a democracy she did not have universal suffrage, and only about half of those entitled to vote today had that right in 1914. While there was a free press, in that there was no censorship as such, members of

11

the press regarded it as their duty to support the establishment, and the two political parties, Conservative and Liberal, were much closer, both in policy and in the sort of people who became members of parliament, than are the Conservatives and Labour today. So we must judge Haig in the context of his time.

1 - Early Days

There was clearly little to occupy the attention of the inhabitants of Edinburgh in the 1860s, for Douglas Haig was born the eleventh and youngest child of his parents in 1861. It was not a military family, nor was it of the nobility, for Douglas's parents were descended from a Haig who had been excluded from the family's lands in the Lowlands in the 1600s, and they now made a living as whisky distillers, the eponymous brand being finally absorbed by the Diageo conglomerate in the 1990s. Aristocratic they were not, but rich they were, and after a prep school in Edinburgh Douglas was educated as a boarder at Clifton College Bristol. Academically he was a slow starter and as an asthmatic he had to struggle to keep up both scholastically and on the sports field. He always had to be careful with his health, but seems to have conquered his asthma, and proved his latent intellectual ability by coming top in Latin in his final year. From school he went on to Brasenose College Oxford in 1880, and while the entrance examination was less rigorous than it is now, it was no walkover either. Today it is fashionable in some quarters to criticise those who are the products of a public school and Oxford, but while opposition to the concept of private schooling is a legitimate viewpoint, it cannot be denied that the system does confer a sound, and broad, academic education. Douglas excelled at sport at Oxford, representing not only the university at polo but also England against the USA (England won), and he was a capable player of the relatively recently codified game of rugby, besides being elected to the Bullingdon Club, now perhaps better known for the propensity of its members to throw bread rolls at each other in restaurants, but which was then known as an equestrian sports club. Douglas passed all his examinations at Oxford, thus qualifying academically for a degree, but by leaving a term early did not fulfil the residential requirements. It was not then unusual for young men to study at Oxford but to leave without taking the degree, and in any case he was getting close to the cut off age for entering the army, which he had now decided to do.

**

Douglas Haig sat the entrance examination for the Royal Military College Sandhurst and arrived there in February 1884, aged twenty-two and eight months, rather older than his fellows who had arrived straight from school. Back then Sandhurst trained officers for the Cavalry and the Infantry, with the Royal Military Academy Woolwich training those for the Engineers and Artillery. While today the majority of Sandhurst entrants are university graduates, then it was unusual, but Douglas's experience of Oxford and his relative maturity were probably an advantage, for at the end of the one year course he passed out top of his intake of 129 officer cadets and won the Anson Sword (now the Sword of Honour). A keen and competent horseman it was no surprise that he was commissioned into the 7th Hussars, one of the smarter cavalry regiments. Initially stationed in Aldershot, there was ample opportunity for hunting and polo, but there was a serious side to the peacetime army as well, and Haig, older than the other subalterns and with the Sword of Honour on his wall, was soon marked out as a young man of promise. When the regiment moved to India Haig was appointed as adjutant, effectively the regimental staff officer, responsible for discipline, administration and acting as the commanding officer's eyes and ears, an appointment normally reserved for an officer with considerably more service than Haig. What is clear is that even as a young officer, with no patrons or family influence to help, Douglas was regarded as an able officer with a good career in front of him. Having acted as a junior staff officer and as a temporary ADC to a general, and having survived attacks of typhus and malaria, he returned to England in 1892 as Aide de Camp to the Inspector General of Cavalry, where he was co-opted as the co-author, with Colonel

John French (later Field Marshal Earl French), of a new edition of the Cavalry Drill Manual, the tactical bible for cavalry operations. Very shortly he found himself the sole author, French having been posted to the War Office, and despite being a junior captain Haig's work was well received. He had spent some considerable time in France and in Germany observing their cavalry, and as he spoke good French and reasonable German he received much more cooperation than John French, who spoke neither, would have.

Douglas Haig entered the Staff College at Camberley for a two year course in 1896. The Staff College exists to train officers for senior command and staff appointments, and while it was, and still is, possible to reach high rank in the British Army without attending the Staff College, it would require exceptional ability and a great deal of luck to do so. Haig's critics maintain that he failed the examination and only got there by undue influence – one claim even has it that he only got a vacancy through the intervention of his wife, who was a lady in waiting to the Queen. The difficulty about that theory is that he did not meet his future wife until nine years after he went to Staff College! The system for entrance to the Staff College was either by competition or by nomination. All candidates had to take an examination, and those getting more than 50% of the marks in all subjects were described as having 'passed' and automatically secured vacancies, regardless of their arm of the service. Vacancies remaining on each two-year course were then filled by nomination by the Commander-in-Chief (later by the Army Council), who presided over a selection board that looked at all officers who had 'qualified' by getting at least 37.5% in all subjects in the exam. Haig got well over 50% in all subjects except mathematics, where he fell short of the 50%, and so could not get a competitive vacancy. He did get there by the perfectly fair and open process of selection by the board, and given his work on the cavalry manual and annual reports by his superiors both on the staff and at regimental duty, he was fully entitled to a place. There was nothing untoward about it, and the same system is used today except that there are no competitive vacancies, all places being filled by selection from candidates who have passed the examination.

After Staff College, where his only disappointment was in not being elected as master of the Sandhurst and Staff College drag hunt (Allenby, the future victor of Palestine, got it instead), Haig was one of three selected graduates to be seconded to the Egyptian army, which Major General (later Field Marshal Lord) Kitchener was preparing to retake the Sudan from the Dervishes who had occupied the province after an uprising by Sufi Muslims in 1881, and who had eventually killed General

Gordon in Khartoum. During his embarkation leave, that short period granted to everyone posted to a foreign station, Douglas made a point of visiting Enfield so that he could familiarise himself with the British army's latest acquisition – the Maxim machinegun. The British had experimented with the Gatling gun, one of the first genuine machineguns, but being hand cranked it was unreliable and subject to numerous stoppages. Hiram Maxim, an American who later became a naturalised British subject and who was eventually knighted by King Edward VII, had invented a new, water-cooled gun that operated by utilising the recoil produced by a fired round to eject the empty case and load and fire the next round, at a rate of 600 rounds a minute. After several modifications it would become the Vickers Maxim and then the Vickers, the standard British medium machine gun from 1912 until its eventual replacement by the General Purpose Machine Gun in 1964.

On arrival in Egypt Douglas found himself as Bimbashi Haig Bey, bimbashi being the Egyptian equivalent of major and bey an honorific title. He was placed in command of an Egyptian cavalry squadron and began to learn the Egyptian version of Arabic. His first taste of combat was at the Battle of Atbara in April 1898, where, at considerable risk to his own life, he rescued a wounded Egyptian soldier under heavy fire from the Dervishes, who, while not the best shots in the world, did possess a very great number of modern rifles captured from the British years before. Haig's contemporaries thought he should have been awarded the Victoria Cross, the highest British decoration for valour, for that action, but it is probable that a combination of Haig's modesty and the rescue being witnessed only by Egyptians and junior British officers prevented that. His fellow officers of the 7th Hussars did however commission a painting of the event, now in the Huntley collection in Edinburgh.

Haig developed a good relationship with Kitchener during what came to be known as the 'River War' (the best account of which is still that published by the young Winston Churchill in 1899, although it has to be said that Haig, who was after all there, thought it was superficial), and while he liked and respected the Sirdar (Kitchener's title as commander in chief of the Egyptian army) he did not approve of his method of command, which was to go direct to the commanding officers of regiments and battalions, rather than acting through divisional and brigade commanders. Such micromanaging and shortcutting of the normal chain of command was frequently a recipe for chaos, and explains Haig's insistence, when in supreme command later, on the correct channels always being followed, and his reluctance to interfere with a subordinate's plan once it had been approved.

19

Following the re-conquest of the Sudan, Haig returned to his regiment as a squadron commander and was then posted to Aldershot as the Brigade Major of the cavalry brigade. The Brigade Major (now the chief of staff) is the senior staff officer of a brigade and only officers considered to be highly competent and to be going places are appointed as such. It was with the cavalry brigade that Haig renewed his long association with the Brigade's commander, Major General John French. French was then an up and coming, dashing field commander, not the fat old blimp that we perhaps think of him now. As an incorrigible womaniser he had been extraordinarily lucky to avoid cashiering (sacking) several times in his career, having been suspected of an affair with his commanding officer's wife as a subaltern, cited in a divorce case by a brother officer, and believed to have had what was then coyly described as 'criminal conversation' with the wife of an Anglo-Indian railway official when commanding his regiment in India. Fortunately for him French's superiors, while strongly disapproving of his behaviour, considered that his inherent ability as a leader merited his being retained in the army rather than being got rid of.

Not only was French incapable of keeping his willy in his trousers, he was also an unsuccessful speculator on the stock exchange. He had made a number of foolish investments which had gone wrong and his creditors were closing in: bankruptcy loomed and with it disgrace and removal from the army. Knowing that Haig was independently rich French approached him for help. This cannot have been easy for either party; it was, and is, an offence in Military Law to borrow from a subordinate or to lend to a superior, but in Haig's letter to his solicitors authorising the loan he makes it clear that in his opinion it would not have been in the army's interests to lose John French – and judging by French's performance in South Africa, Haig was right.

Soon the Cavalry Brigade was off to South Africa. During the Boer war Haig was firstly a staff officer in a brigade, which was then a division where although considered too junior to be chief of staff, as an officer of proven ability he found himself deferred to by the rest of the staff and effectively was the chief. In 1901 he commanded a mobile column and was then promoted to lieutenant colonel, and, as there was no vacancy in his own regiment, the 7th Hussars, he was given command of the 17th Lancers, also in South Africa. Douglas Haig was now forty years old, the normal age at the time for promotion to lieutenant colonel, but he reached that rank after only sixteen years commissioned service, which was very rapid progress indeed, and without a military background or an old boy network to rely on. It is true that he was rich, but success in the

British army could not and cannot be bought, and in any case it was rare at the time for any cavalry officer not to have a private income. It is also interesting to note that of those sixteen years Haig had spent two years at the Staff College, three years officially on the staff and a year or so as a temporary staff officer and ADC, with ten years at regimental duty in command of soldiers. Today, unless one was very lucky, the breakdown would be more heavily weighted towards the staff.

It was from the rank of lieutenant colonel that Haig's career really took off. He became a brevet colonel in 1902 (a way of rewarding someone who deserved promotion but where there was no vacancy in that rank). He therefore was paid as a colonel but continued doing a lieutenant colonel's job as commanding officer of his regiment. In October 1902 he and the regiment returned to the UK from South Africa and in 1903 with Haig the captain of the team, the regiment won the Inter Regimental polo tournament, hotly contested then as it still is now. In that same year Kitchener (now General Viscount), recently appointed Commander-in-Chief, India, asked for Haig as his Inspector General of Cavalry. Haig thus became a local and then substantive Major General at the age of 42. In India he supported Kitchener in his root and branch reform of the Indian Army, designed to turn what was really a colonial gendarmerie into a professional army that could be deployed anywhere in the world.

In 1905 Haig went home to England on leave and, along with a number of other generals, was invited to Windsor to stay with the King for Ascot Week. The British monarch is the Commander in Chief of the Armed Forces, and successive monarchs have made and do make a point of getting to know senior officers. King Edward VII certainly knew of Haig from reports on the Sudan and Boer wars, and would almost certainly have met him during the frequent royal visits to military units. The king would, of course, have been particularly interested to meet the then youngest major general in the British army. On the Thursday evening Haig was introduced to Dorothy Vivian, maid of honour to the Queen. On Friday he played golf with her and on the Saturday he proposed and she accepted! It was a whirlwind romance but it does seem that Haig, whose life so far was bounded by the professional, leavened by hunting, polo and golf, fell totally in love with this spirited, intelligent and very pretty young lady who could ride almost as well as he could, and played a mean game of golf too. It was certainly not a marriage of convenience – both were of independent means. It was an incredibly happy marriage and Dorothy (Doris) was completely supportive of Douglas for the rest of his life, and worked tirelessly to protect his reputation and to advance the

23

cause of the British Legion long after his death. There was an age gap – he was 44, she 25 – and when Douglas went to ask Doris' mother for her daughter's hand in marriage, her mother refused to receive him, so he just camped on her doorstep until she did. Newly married Haig and his wife returned to India, but were then summoned home the following year, in 1906, when he was asked for by the Secretary of State for War, Haldane.

Richard Haldane, a forty-nine year old lawyer, had been appointed Secretary of State for War by Sir Henry Campbell-Bannerman, prime minister of a Liberal minority government, and retained that post after the Liberals won a landslide victory in the general election of 1906. Haldane was a reformer and intended to continue the process of reforming the army, and to a lesser extent the navy, begun by Cardwell and carried on by Childers and Esher. He realised that the regular army needed to be transformed from a colonial police force, very good at dealing with rebellious natives and cheeky tribal potentates, but ill prepared for a war against a first class enemy, into one capable of taking on a sophisticated opponent. Furthermore, as a professional, all volunteer force in a nation implacably opposed to the continental practice of conscription as being an unacceptable imposition on a free born Englishman, there were no reserves worthy of the name, only the frightfully patriotic but militarily useless regiments of militia, volunteers and yeoman cavalry. But to put the army on a sound footing able to intervene in high intensity warfare anywhere in the world, Haldane needed a right hand man who was of the military, respected by it and young enough and vigorous enough to push through the much needed reforms against entrenched opposition from those elements of the army that opposed change on principle. That man was Major General Douglas Haig.

The Esher reforms had already established a permanent general staff, with the professional head of the army as the Chief of the General Staff (CIGS) rather than the commander in chief, the last of whom was Lord Roberts. The word 'imperial' was inserted in the title to make the point that the dominion armies too were to organise and equip themselves the same as the British Army. There was, however, no permanent expeditionary force; that is a formation ready and able to deploy anywhere in the world with all its supporting arms and dedicated transport. If a force was to be sent abroad then the Horse Guards (equivalent to the Ministry of Defence today) allocated units to it and officers were found to provide the staff. Haldane and Haig between them created the Expeditionary Force. Of one cavalry and six infantry divisions it was equipped, trained and made ready for war with commanders and staff officers appointed. While ultimately the British

Expeditionary Force would deploy to Belgium on the outbreak of the First World War, it was designed to go anywhere in the world, although increasingly Germany, rather than France or Russia, was seen as being the probable enemy should a major war break out. To provide a reserve for the regular army, the pair created the Territorial Force (later the Territorial Army, now the Army Reserves) which was a transformation of the volunteers, Militia and Yeomanry from weekend drinking clubs with considerable social cachet but little competence into a nation-wide military organisation to be equipped and organised as for the regular army. The primary role of the Territorial Force was to release regular units, including the Expeditionary Force, to go abroad, and its secondary role was to provide reinforcements.

Additionally, and in the teeth of opposition from the bean counters, Haldane and Haig ensured that the army was provided with the best weapons and equipment that could be obtained. The short Magazine Lee Enfield had been issued to the infantry and the cavalry from 1906, and was probably in terms of ballistics the best military rifle ever, remaining in service until 1960. An improved form of web equipment was developed and the artillery was provided with the 13 pounder for the horse artillery, the eighteen pounder and the 4.5" howitzer for the field artillery and the sixty pounder for the heavies.

Again, surprisingly perhaps, the British army had no overall doctrine, with individual commanders being left to decide on how best to do things. This was all very well for minor colonial brushfire campaigns involving only a few battalions, but could not work if the army was involved in a major war. Haig wanted to put this right, and the result was Field Service Regulations, laying down how the army would train for and fight its wars. It covered everything from communications to cooking and from embarking on ships to the ranges of artillery; it laid down the general principles for each phase of war: the advance, the attack, defence and the withdrawal as well as dealing with reconnaissance and outpost duty and listing what equipment and stores units needed on mobilisation. It was designed to ensure that all formations of the army, and all arms (cavalry, engineers, artillery and infantry), had a universal doctrine that would allow them to train and operate under common principles. Haldane was the political driving force, ensuring that the army was kept out of politics and sidestepping those like Lloyd-George and Churchill who wanted to reduce the defence budget, while Haig provided the military and organisational brain. It was the most radical and far reaching reform in a generation, and if Haldane had been assisted by a general of less intelligence or less foresight, then the result of the First World War might have been very different.

After the War Office in 1909, and now knighted as a result of his work with Haldane, Haig was off to India again, as chief of staff of the Indian Army and promoted to lieutenant general. Here he continued the modernisation programme begun by Kitchener, and by the time his tour was over the Indian cavalry were probably the best in the world, as they would show on the Western Front in due course. Having been created a Knight Commander of the Indian Empire by King George V at the Delhi Durbar of 1911, in 1912 Sir Douglas and Lady Haig were on the move again, this time back to England and to the command at Aldershot. Aldershot was the most important, and the most prestigious, command in the UK army, and most of the units stationed there were allocated to the Expeditionary Force, so if that force was deployed then the General officer Commanding, Haig, would go too. As far as Haig was concerned the army in Aldershot might be at peace, but they would prepare for war, and apart from Sundays when he would play golf (after church, of course) and the occasional days hunting or polo mid-week, Douglas put in long hours ensuring that the troops were ready for whatever might happen, for it was clear to most senior officers, and to some politicians too, that war was coming and that it would be war with Germany. With other officers of the Expeditionary Force he travelled to France for unofficial talks with the French general staff, including

Joffre, the commander in chief of the French Army, and Foch, a senior commander, and such liaison visits would be of immense help when the moment came. It is interesting to note that in 1914 the Dover to Calais ferry, which Haig used regularly to get to France, took one hour for the crossing: now it takes an hour and a half!

***

On 29 June 1914 the Archduke Franz Ferdinand, heir to the throne of Austria Hungary, was assassinated in Sarajevo, Bosnia, by a Serbian nationalist. Austria issued an ultimatum to Serbia demanding the arrest of those responsible, the dismissal of anti-Austrian elements in the Serbian civil service and the media and demanding that Austrian troops be permitted to enter Serbia to root out those seen as supporting the assassination. Serbia agreed to all demands except the last, and on 28 July Austria Hungary, egged on by her ally Germany, declared war on Serbia. Russia, as the self-proclaimed protector of all Slavs, mobilised her armed forces; France, allied to Russia, did the same, as did Germany and, fearing she would be in the way of any Franco German conflict, so did Belgium. On 3 August German troops invaded Belgium. Belgium appealed for British assistance and on 4 August, no reply having been received to a demand that Germany withdraw, Britain declared war on Germany.

The British Expeditionary Force, commanded by Field Marshal Sir John French and consisting of two corps, I Corps commanded by Haig and II Corps by Lieutenant General Sir James Grierson, began to move to the southern English ports to embark for France. Haig had been marked out for high command from an early age. In all his many appointments, whether in command of a squadron of 100 men as a young major or heading a mobile column and then a regiment, or in his staff appointments, he had excelled. That the British Expeditionary Force was said, correctly, then and now, to have been the best led, the best trained and the best equipped body of troops ever to have left these shores, was very largely due to the work Haig had done under Haldane, and his preparations of his troops while in command at Aldershot. His greatest test was now to begin.

2 - To War

While the British government did not decide until relatively late in the day that they would support the French on land, as opposed to at sea, unofficial planning by French and British officers had been taking place during the years leading up to 1914. It was said, possibly apocryphally, that Major General Henry Wilson, Director of Military Operations at the War Office and the driving force behind the 'Support the French' school, asked Joffre how many British soldiers he would need in the event of war, to which the reply was 'one, and we will ensure that he is killed on the first day'. The point was that the French wanted a commitment from the British, which they could only be certain of if British troops were deployed to the continent.

The French had come up with Plan XVII in the event of war with Germany, which saw the French army concentrating on the Belgian and German frontiers and attacking into Alsace Lorraine and Belgium. Alsace and a third of Lorraine had been lost by France to Germany in the war of 1870 and so there was a certain amount – some might say a very large amount – of revanchist wishful thinking in the plan, which was popular with French politicians if not with all the French generals. In accordance with that plan the British Expeditionary Force (BEF) would move into France short of the Belgian border and take post on the left of the French Fifth Army. As soon as war was declared the British army called up its reserves, those soldiers who had completed a regular engagement and who had returned to civilian life with a reserve commitment in event of war, ranging from five years to ten years from discharge, depending on their arm of the service. Once these reserves had been absorbed, bringing cavalry regiments up to a strength of twenty-five officers and 526 Other Ranks, and infantry battalions to thirty officers and 992 OR, the BEF began to move across to France, by ship to the channel ports and then by rail to Mauberge in France, ready to move into Belgium. Douglas himself crossed on 15 August and on 17th the commander of II Corps, Lieutenant General Grierson, fifty-five years old but grossly overweight and unfit, had a massive heart attack on a French train and died. His replacement was General Sir Horace Smith-Dorrien.

The German plan for 1914 was drawn up to avoid the nightmare of every German politician and general – a war on two fronts. German military thinking was therefore devoted to fighting on one front at a time and winning quickly. As the

Germans thought that Russian mobilisation and deployments would take much longer than that of the French (not true as it turned out) then they would deal with France first before turning on Russia. France was to be defeated by the Schlieffen Plan, originally drawn up by that archetypal staff officer Count Alfred von Schlieffen and promulgated in 1905. Amended several times since, it envisaged enticing the French to advance into Germany in the centre and south into what Schlieffen called his 'mousetrap', while the main body of the German army would launch a massive sweep down the Channel coast, curving round to the west of Paris and pinning the French army against its own frontiers and destroying it. As the Germans had to win a war quickly else they risk not winning it at all, this was planned to take six weeks.

Professionally far more capable than ally or enemy force the BEF undoubtedly was, but it was pitifully small: four infantry divisions compared to sixty-two French, and one cavalry division to ten French ones. Haig felt strongly that the BEF should be held back in England to train a much larger army which could then intervene and bring the war to an end 'before we are financially exhausted' as he put it, but the French wanted British support now and given the assurances that had been given, unofficial though most of them were, there was no political alternative to sending the troops as soon as possible after the outbreak of war. Haig had no option but to accept that reasoning. Given the size of the BEF, once it had been committed Field Marshal French had to fall in with the French plans and so once the Germans had breached Belgian neutrality the BEF moved north into Belgium too, keeping pace with General Charles Lanrezac's French Fifth army on its right. Running into German advance guards north of Mons the BEF dug in along the Mons canal. On the left of the BEF was the Groupe D'Amade, three French divisions of elderly reservists trying to cover the seventy miles from Mons north to the Channel. Smith-Dorrien's II Corps was positioned along the canal to the west of Mons, while Haig's I Corps took post to the north and east of the town along the canal and then off to the south east.

Matters were not helped by the mutual dislike of the British commander-in-chief and General Lanrezac. Neither spoke the other's language; Lanrezac resented the English, who were after all his nation's hereditary enemy, and French thought the French untrustworthy and unhygienic. It was not a good start. To the French, whose Plan XVII was failing spectacularly in what became known as the Battle of the Frontiers, and in the context of the war as a whole the Battle of Mons is not much more than a footnote, but it was the blooding of the BEF, for on Sunday 23 August the full weight of the Schlieffen plan fell on the left wing of the Anglo French line, with the main thrust on Smith Dorrien's II Corps. The corps was grossly outnumbered, with, eventually, ten infantry and three cavalry divisions opposed to them, but the position held, largely due to the excellent marksmanship of the professional British infantry and the accurate shelling of the eighteen pounders. Haig's I Corps were far less heavily pressed and were able to hold their line and support II Corps where they could. By mid-afternoon, despite a heroic defence by the infantry of II Corps, numbers began to tell, and when the Germans, despite heavy losses, managed to capture two of the bridges over the canal Smith Dorrien had no option but to pull his troops back to a secondary defence position three miles to the south. After nightfall the two divisions of I Corps were able to cover the withdrawal of the last units of II Corps and then to withdraw themselves. The BEF was now holding a frontage of about seventeen miles.

It was around dusk on 23 August that Sir John French discovered that the French Fifth Army had withdrawn from their positions and were now well to his south. French claimed that Lanrezac had deliberately ordered the withdrawal of his army without telling the British, although it is perhaps more likely that in the fog of war telephone lines were cut, runners got captured and ADCs got lost. Whatever the reason, the failure to communicate only added to French's dislike and distrust of his allies. With the French Fifth Army in retreat and the Groupe d'Armade also pulling back at a rapid rate, French now had to withdraw the BEF, although he claimed that he could have held had the Fifth Army remained in position. In fact, while one good little one may well beat three or four not so good big ones, he will not beat ten big ones, and in any case the German army was a well-oiled fighting machine, even if individually many of its soldiers were not a match for the British professionals. Now, with both flanks open and unprotected the BEF risked being enveloped and destroyed: at this stage of the war the British only had one army, and if they broke it there was not yet another to be had.

***

On 25 August the retreat from Mons began, when the BEF, co-operating with their French allies withdrew 200 miles to the south of the River Marne (which they crossed on 3 September) and which went on until 5 September, an average of seventeen miles a day, which given that most of the force were on their feet and had to move tactically, was pretty good going. That the men were able to maintain that pace and were fed and supplied during it was due to the foresight and planning of the Quartermaster General of the BEF, Major General Sir William Robertson, who had foreseen an eventual retreat and had prepositioned dumps of rations, water, forage, medical supplies and ammunition along the likely rearward routes. Robertson was that iconic rebuttal of the accusation that all British officers were born with silver spoons in their mouths, for, as the son of an illegitimate sub postmaster and his illegitimate wife, he left school at thirteen and entered domestic service before enlisting as a private soldier at the age of eighteen. After eleven years in the ranks he had risen to the rank of Troop Sergeant Major (equivalent to Staff Sergeant) and was commissioned as a second lieutenant. He would eventually be the professional head of the army as CIGS, a field marshal and a baronet.

Douglas Haig's I Corps was relatively unscathed during the retreat, having to fight only minor rearguard actions. This was not the case with II Corps, where Smith Dorrien had to fight the battle of Le Cateau on 26 August, to hand off the pursuing Germans and give himself time to outdistance them. Not only did relations between Lanrezac in particular and the French commanders in general and Sir John French worsen during the retreat, but Haig, who had hitherto loyally supported his superior despite having a less than high opinion of his command of the BEF, now came in for the rough edge of French's tongue. On 28 August Joffre ordered Lanrezac to cease withdrawing and to turn his army about and attack the advancing Germans. Haig contacted Lanrezac and offered to help with his two divisions. This would have made a considerable difference to the eventual outcome, but when Field Marshal French heard of it he sent an angry telegram to Haig demanding to know what Commander I Corps thought he was doing; that he was not to play any part in the coming operation, not even by using his artillery, and that no such offers were to be made in future without the express permission of the Commander in Chief BEF. Haig protested, but got nowhere, and his corps sat idle while the French counter attacked. Haig's doubts as to French's fitness for command were only reinforced by this extraordinary and petty decision.

Meanwhile the Schlieffen Plan was running out of steam. The German army simply couldn't march fast enough, the removal of the Netherlands from the original plan (the current chief of staff, Moltke, thought that invading one neutral country, Belgium, was quite enough) and the breakdown of the logistical chain meant that the plan was already way behind schedule. Instead of wheeling to the west of Paris, the German armies now wheeled to the east of that city, and Joffre saw his opportunity. So happened the Battle of the Marne, probably the critical battle of the whole war, for if it had been lost the Germans would have been in Paris and the British would have withdrawn to cover the Channel ports. Fought from 5 to 12 September 1914 it almost happened without the British, for on 30 August French decided that his army could take no more and proposed withdrawing them from the line, marching them off to the other side of the River Seine – which he thought would take ten days – for rest and recuperation. This was despite knowing that III Corps, one of the two divisions of the Expeditionary Force that had been left behind in England (possible trouble in Ireland and a fear of a German invasion being cited as the reasons, the former unlikely and the latter utterly fanciful) were on the way to join him. French did not tell Joffre of his plans, but fortunately he did tell the Secretary of State for War (minister of defence), Field Marshal Lord Kitchener, the first soldier of the Empire and brought into the cabinet on the outbreak of war, who rushed over to France in full uniform to put some steel into French's backbone, order him unequivocally to conform to the French plans and reassure Joffre that Britain would not desert them.

The Battle of the Marne pushed the Germans back to the River Aisne, and now began the 'race to the sea', not really a race but an attempt by both sides to outflank the other, and thus moving farther and farther north until the allies won, just, by getting to Newport on the Belgian coast. The BEF moved up to Belgian Flanders where I Corps and Haig were ordered by French to advance and capture Bruges. This was an entirely unrealistic plan which could not possible succeed, and while Haig's men did capture Ypres they found themselves on the receiving end of a determined German assault to break through and get to the Channel ports. There was little tactical importance in the town of Ypres, indeed it would have been far better to abandon it and defend along higher ground farther west, but Ypres was the only Belgian town of any significance not occupied by the Germans and politically it had to be held. Again and again German infantry attacked all around what had now become a salient, and Haig was frequently seen cantering his horse forward to the threatened areas with shells bursting all around him.

The First Battle of Ypres was a close run thing, with dismounted cavalry fighting as infantry, and only the arrival of five brigades of Indian infantry at Marseilles in September enabled Haig to fill the gaps in the thin and stretched line. By mid-November the situation had stabilised but now the war of movement, which everybody had trained for and expected, was over, and both sides settled down into what was effectively siege warfare, with ever more elaborate trench systems running all the way from the Belgian coast to the Swiss border. The northernmost twelve miles would be held by the Belgians, the next thirty-five miles by the BEF and a staggering 342 miles by the French. Although the BEF as it expanded would extend its frontage, this would be the situation for the next three and a half years, as both sides sought ways of breaking through the defences of the other. Once the chaos of First Ypres was over, chaos that Haig managed well, with units being fed into the battle as they arrived, the BEF took up the line from the north of the Ypres salient to the La Bassée Canal with, running from north to south, III Corps, the newly arrived IV Corps, I Corps, II Corps and the Indian Corps, with the Cavalry Corps in support in the rear.

In December 1914 the BEF had expanded to consist of four British and one Indian corps, while the cavalry had expanded to one British and one Indian corps. It was therefore decided to reorganise the BEF into two armies. First Army with I, IV and the Indian Corps would be commanded by Haig, promoted to full general, and Second Army with II and III Corps plus an independent division by Smith-Dorrien. But it was the winter of 1914 that saw the last hurrah of the old regular army. Casualties on the retreat from Mons, the battles on the Aisne and in the First Battle of Ypres (there would be two more) and the need to man training units with regulars meant that increasingly the British army would be composed of the 'New Armies', Territorials and, from mid-1916, conscripts. On Kitchener's appointment as Secretary of State at the outbreak of war he had told the Cabinet that the war would last for three years and that he would need a million men. The politicians were aghast, but even Kitchener was being optimistic, for the war lasted four and a quarter years and nine million men from Britain and the Empire would be mobilised by its end. Kitchener asked for recruits to the relatively tiny regular army, and these volunteers were formed into battalions of the 'New Armies', but while the material was in general excellent, it would take time to train and equip them, and the finding of Non Commissioned Officers (NCOs) and officers to lead them would increasingly be a problem. Private soldiers can be trained in a matter of weeks; officers and NCOs have to be grown. Inevitably standards would drop, at least in the short term.

***

As an army commander Douglas Haig's first major battle was that of Neuve Chapelle in March 1915. Neuve Chapelle was a French village in the centre of a salient that jutted into British held territory. If that salient could be nipped out the front would be shortened and the village could then act as a springboard for an attack on Aubers Ridge, a dominating feature that overlooked a large part of the British line. Haig's plan was for a preliminary artillery bombardment to destroy the German wire followed by a pincer attack by two divisions, the Indian Meerut Division and the British 8th Division. In the event the British division could make little progress on the first day due to their artillery failing to cut the wire and a particularly well-fortified German strong point, but the Gurkhas and Garhwalis between them broke through the German lines, took the village and by last light had consolidated their position and were ready to move on towards the ridge. Events conspired against them. Attacks the next day were constantly postponed because of the weather, and when that cleared the British still had problems coming up on the Indian's left, although between them they beat off a massive German counter attack by Bavarian reserve divisions (including lance corporal Adolf Hitler). After four days Haig closed the battle down. Aubers Ridge had not been captured and Haig has been criticised for not persevering. The bald facts are that he could not have persevered. During the battle the artillery had fired off 112,000 shells and the infantry had fired around three million rounds. That scale of expenditure had never been envisaged during pre-war planning, and there was simply not enough ammunition to continue the battle. As it was, the German line had been pushed back 1000 yards over a frontage of two miles and the Germans had suffered far more in dead and wounded than their attackers. Haig was right to close the battle when he did.

The next major battle for the British was the Second Battle of Ypres in April and May 1915, when the Germans launched the first gas attack against the Ypres Salient. Douglas had little part to play, except in despatching one of his Indian divisions as a reinforcement for Second Army, but the battle did lead to the effective sacking of Smith-Dorrien. Bad blood between him and French went back to the Boer War, and French did not want him as a corps and later army commander. Smith-Dorrien's advice during Second Ypres that the British should pull back to a more easily defendable line was militarily sound but politically unacceptable, and French, still smarting over Smith-Dorrien's fighting at Le Cateau which French claimed (wrongly) was unnecessary, saw his chance and Smith-Dorrien went, replaced by Lieutenant General Sir Herbert Plumer, promoted to full general. It has to be said that Smith-Dorrien had a ferocious temper, and if one is cleverer than one's superior it is a good rule not to let that become obvious to the superior.

Sir John French's last major battle as the commander of the BEF, and Haig's last as an army commander, was the battle of Loos in September 1915. This was the largest battle the British had yet engaged in, although it was only a very small part of a much larger French offensive, the battles of Champagne and Artois, which required the British to advance against high ground covering the German occupied Loos en Gohelle and Lens, industrial and mining towns dotted with slag heaps and mine pit heads, over a frontage of eight miles. Haig, to whose First Army, now of four corps, the task was given, immediately set out to look at the ground and prepare an outline plan. His findings were stark: the whole of the area was overlooked by the Germans who were on the high ground in well dug in positions; the ground between the opposing front lines was open and devoid of cover; the assembly of the necessary troops would be bound to be discovered by the Germans who could bombard forming up places and supply dumps. His conclusion was that the attack could only be feasible if a very great deal of artillery could be employed (and that amount of artillery did not yet exist), and even then there would be very hard hand to hand fighting as the British troops forced their way through the German trench lines. French, who had originally agreed to fall in with his ally's plans, now accepted Haig's recommendations, but once again politics intervened: it was essential to support the French and Sir John and Sir Douglas were ordered by Kitchener to get on with it.

Seeking for some way to counter the difficulties of advancing over such unfavourable ground, the British decided to use gas for the first time. After the German gas attack at Ypres in April the British had made a great fuss, claiming that its use was contrary to the laws of war as enunciated in the Hague Convention of 1907, which all the participants of the war had signed up to. Having made their protests, the British opened a factory in Wembley and began to make gas themselves. The outline plan for the Loos offensive was for an artillery bombardment to try to destroy or at least damage the German defences, co-ordinated with bombing of road junctions and supply dumps behind the German lines by aircraft of the Royal Flying Corps, after which 150 tons of chlorine gas would be released from 5,500 cylinders. As the gas wafted across no-man's-land towards the Germans it would be followed by the infantry, who were equipped with a much more efficient form of gas mask than were their opponents. As the gas attack would depend on the wind blowing in the right direction, that is west to east towards the German lines, Haig recommended that if the wind was not favourable and gas could not be used, then the attack should be postponed until it was. This was not acceptable to the French who insisted that the British attack must go ahead along with their own offensive on 25 September 1915.

Haig's plan saw the initial attack being made with six divisions, three regular, at least in name but with a high proportion of recruits just out of training, one Territorial and two New Army, the first time New Army formations would be used. In reserve would be another three divisions, the Guards (regular) and two New Army. A British division and an Indian division would mount a diversionary attack north of the main attack to prevent the Germans moving reserves south. The purpose of a reserve was and is to capitalise on success, to bolster up weaknesses, to reinforce and to deal with the unexpected. A commander without a reserve cannot influence the battle, and it was handling of the reserves that precipitated a major disagreement between Haig and his superior, French. Haig wanted the reserves to be well forward so that they would be available swiftly if required, and to be under his command. French demurred: he would retain control of the reserves. Normally the officer in command of the operation, in this case Haig, would have the reserves under command and would decide when and where they should be used, but it was not and is not unreasonable for the overall commander – in this case French – to keep them in his gift in case of a crisis elsewhere. It was however agreed that should Haig ask for the reserves they would be released to him.

In the event at 0550 hours on 25 September the wind was blowing in more or less the right direction. The gas was released and the infantry began to move behind it. In the north the wind soon eddied and was of little help, but in the south some real progress was made with the German first line overrun. Now was the time to put in the reserves to carry the attack forward, but although Haig asked for them at 0700 hours a failure in communications with French, who had established himself in a tactical headquarters without the road and telephone facilities of his main headquarters, combined with traffic control problems on the way up, meant that when the reserves did arrive, at around 1800 hours, it was far too late, and in any case only one of the three divisions – the Guards – was capable of doing anything very much. The battle went on until 18 October, and while some progress was made – Loos was now in British hands and their front line pushed forward by almost two miles – the breakthrough never came and the casualty list was enormous. Amongst the dead were three of the nine divisional commanders (major generals), giving the lie to the belief that all generals spent the war miles behind the lines. The failure to provide the reserves when needed (and in fairness to French it must be said that being of only three divisions they may not have made a huge difference) caused great displeasure in London and in the BEF, and all added to increasing doubts as to Sir John French's fitness for command. Enquiries were made by Kitchener in London and by the King's secretary, Lord Stampfordham, and while Haig had been brought up in a school where you did not sneak and where loyalty to a superior was paramount, when asked directly by Robertson, now chief of staff of the BEF, relaying an enquiry from Kitchener, to state his views on the handling of the reserves, he had little choice but to do so. In fact, as Haig (and French) realised, the Territorials were only partly experienced while the New Army divisions were only partly trained and while of excellent material were severely lacking in officers and NCOs with any experience at all. These too were major contributory factors to the failure to effect a genuine rupture of the German defences. Withal, confidence in French was ebbing fast, both in London and in the BEF, and the sacking of Smith-Dorrien, and the unchivalrous manner in which it had been done, still rankled amongst Smith-Dorrien's supporters, of which there were many. Lord Haldane, now out of office but used by the government as a trouble shooter, arrived on the Western Front and asked Haig directly to state his assessment of French. Having skirted round the subject Haig gave Haldane, whom he knew well from their time at the War Office together, his honest opinion that French should go, but that his exit should be an honourable one.

In mid-December Lord Esher arrived as an emissary of the Prime Minister and asked French to tender his resignation as commander of the BEF. As a sop he would be raised to the peerage as an earl and given command of Home Forces. There were only two possible replacements: Haig or Robertson. In the event Haig was appointed as commander in chief BEF and Robertson on promotion to full general was recalled to England as CIGS, the professional head of the army. In the first year of the war Haig's command had risen from two divisions to fourteen divisions and a cavalry divisions. Now it was to expand even further.

3 - Sir Douglas Haig's Command

Between August 1914 and early 1916 the BEF grew from one army of two infantry corps of four infantry divisions with one cavalry division, or slightly less than 100,000 men, to four armies with eighteen infantry corps and fifty-eight infantry divisions and two cavalry corps of five cavalry divisions, or rather more than a million men. By the middle of 1916 it would be one and a half million. Haig's own span of command increased thirty-seven times, from forty thousand men in 1914 to one and a half million in 1916. Armies are organised on the basis of the largest number of men one man can directly command, and the largest number of units that one headquarters can control. All armies organised themselves in roughly the same way, and the Roman organisation of the conturbium – century – cohort – legion is not dissimilar to the platoon – company – battalion – brigade of modern times. The workhorse of BEF was the infantry, with its basic brick the section of ten men commanded by a corporal. Four sections made a platoon commanded by a second lieutenant or lieutenant with a sergeant to assist him. Four platoons made a company commanded by a captain or major and four companies made a battalion, commanded by a lieutenant colonel. The battalion was part of a regiment, but while in the French and German (and American) armies the regiment was a tactical formation, with all its battalions operating together, in the British army the regiment was an administrative grouping. The men in its various battalions all wore the same badge in their headgear and probably came from the same part of the country, but the battalions might be spread all over the world, with the 1st battalion in India, the 2nd in the BEF and the 3rd in Gibraltar. Regiments usually had a territorial title (The Lancashire Fusiliers, The Royal Irish Rifles) unless it was a Guards battalion (The Coldstream Guards, The Welsh Guards) or one of those regiments that recruited nationwide like the Rifle Brigade (confusingly, not a brigade but a regiment of four battalions in 1914). Other arms were similarly organised. The battalion was the soldier's family and it was to the battalion that his loyalty lay, any larger formation being simply referred to by most private soldiers as 'them'. Four battalions constituted a brigade, commanded by a brigadier general; there were three brigades in a division plus a cavalry squadron, artillery, engineer, medical and transport units. A corps comprised of two or more divisions and was usually commanded by a

51

lieutenant general, and an army contained two or more corps and was commanded by a general.

It was not only the hugely expanded manpower of the BEF that Haig inherited at the end of 1915, but it was now increasingly diverse. New units had been created: the Machine Gun Corps, which took the Vickers guns away from battalions and concentrated them in machine gun companies and battalions; Trench Mortar batteries, Royal Engineers Tunnelling Companies (eventually twenty-four of them each about 1000 men strong) who fought their almost private war deep underground; Chemical Companies, responsible for launching gas attacks and providing protection from them; anti-aircraft artillery units; Signals units responsible for establishing and maintaining communications, aircraft flown by army and naval pilots and increasingly motor transport units replacing the reliance on horse power. Although the Indian Corps had left Europe for Mesopotamia at the end of 1915, Canadian, New Zealand and Australian divisions had arrived as had a South African brigade and a battalion from Newfoundland, not yet part of the Dominion of Canada. With the enormous expansion of the fighting elements came an inevitable increase in the logistic tail, with depots set up behind the lines to supply and maintain them. The length of front too had expanded from twenty miles in August 1914 to eighty miles, from the north of the Ypres salient to the River Somme, in early 1916. Douglas Haig was now responsible not only for fighting the war on the Western Front, but for the training, supplying, maintaining, moving, welfare and morale of the biggest army the British had ever put in the field – or ever would put in the field. He was responsible to the home government for the handling of its army and to the French and Belgian governments in relation to administrative matters in their territory and had to liaise with the French and Belgian and eventually American military commanders in regard to the conduct of the war. Never before or since has so much responsibility been placed upon one man.

To exercise command and control over this huge organisation required a headquarters, and as one man could not possibly do everything, that headquarters had to have a team of staff officers to ensure that the commander's wishes were carried out. In 1914 General Headquarters (GHQ) of the BEF had fifty-three staff officers and by January 1916 that had risen to 101, or by a much smaller factor than the troops for whom they were responsible. A common criticism of commanders at all levels in the First World War is that they were remote from their men, ensconced in comfortable chateaux miles behind the lines and having no idea of conditions at the front. Once trench warfare became a permanent reality there were generally three lines of trenches: the forward trench, known as the firing line, the support trench behind that, and the reserve trench farther to the rear. The idea was to establish a defence in depth: if the enemy succeeded in breaking through the firing line he would then come up against the support line, and in the unlikely event of penetrating that he would then have the reserve line to deal with. The reality is that apart from the very smallest groups a commander could not possibly exert command and control from the front line trench. A platoon commander, whose forty men might hold fifty yards of front, could be in the firing line with his men and almost always was. The company commander, whose company would hold a hundred yards of front with two platoons in the front line and two in the support or reserve trenches would base himself where he could get to any of his platoons if necessary, while a battalion commander, holding perhaps five hundred yards with two of his companies forward and two back would have his battalion headquarters in the support or reserve trench. Again, a brigade commander would be overseeing four battalions and could not possible do that from the firing line, and would be stationed somewhere behind the reserve line. The key was communications. Within the platoon, voice or whistle would suffice, above that the telephone and the runner enabled superiors to obtain information from those under their command and to issue instructions to them. The larger the command the more important this became. A divisional commander had to be able to talk to his three brigades, his cavalry squadron, his engineers, his artillery, and Royal Flying Corps units in support as well as being able to communicate with the relevant corps headquarters and corps staff. Each division did have a radio, primitive by modern standards, not easily moved and needing constant nursing to work. Not only did he have to have telephone and radio communication the divisional commander had to have road access, stabling for the prime movers of the day – horses – and accommodation for his staff. He needed somewhere to plan, to brief, to hold conferences, to lay out large scale maps, and all this could only be done in a sprawling tent village or by taking over a suitable building already in place – a large manor house or a chateau and it had to be beyond field artillery range.

Because a commander had his headquarters well behind the lines did not mean that he was ignorant of matters at the front. At all levels commanders went forward and visited their units in the trenches, where they could be brought up to date with the current situation, assess capabilities and measure morale. As we have seen, one third of the major generals involved in the Battle of Loos were killed, and in the course of the war no fewer than ninety-seven British generals were killed – and killed by enemy action – while another 146 were wounded or captured.

Whatever else they were doing they were not skulking miles behind the lines.

In the early days of the BEF, once the war of movement had come to an end, Sir John French had his GHQ at St Omer. On assuming supreme command and after extending the British front south, Haig moved the main headquarters to Montreuil-sur-Mer, which was sixty miles from Ypres at the north end of the British line and sixty miles from the River Somme at the south end. It was fifty miles west of the centre of the British line, seven miles from the main logistics base at Étaples, the largest British base ever constructed overseas, and twenty miles from Boulogne, the main port of entry for men and supplies arriving from the UK. It was also about a hundred miles, or three hours motoring, from the French GHQ at Chantilly. Montreuil had good road communications, an efficient civilian telephone system, a chateau large enough to house the main staff departments and accommodation nearby for staff officers and the various cooks, clerks, signallers, escorts and all those needed to keep the headquarters functioning. It was, in other words, the ideal place to put a headquarters that had to command one and a half million men spread over eighty miles of front. While Haig most certainly did not share the discomfort and the dangers of his men in the front line trenches, he would have been of no earthly use to them if he had: his role was to plan, to direct and to manage and he could not possibly do that from a hole in the ground at the front. He had in any case proved his personal courage in previous wars and battles. A typical day for Haig based in Montreuil might be to rise early (a habit from boyhood) and have a light breakfast and then study the reports that had come in from the front line overnight, cables and telegrams from London and communications from the French and the Belgians, after which he would have briefings from his chief of staff, his chief of intelligence, his senior artillery and engineer officers and the commander of the Royal Flying Corps in France, Brigadier General 'Boom' Trenchard, later known as the father of the Royal Air Force. In the afternoon he would usually visit units at the front, going part of the way by car and then switching to his horse which would be boxed to meet him.

Of course there were soldiers who claimed that they never saw Haig in all the three years of his command, but there were over 700 battalions of infantry alone, to say nothing of cavalry, engineer, artillery and logistic and administrative units, several thousand major units in all. He might, just, manage to visit most of them once during his command but the individual soldier might well be asleep, away, on leave, sick or otherwise not around to see the great man. He did of course visit divisional headquarters more often, but even then there were over sixty infantry divisions and five of cavalry. The only headquarters that he could regularly and frequently visit would be army headquarters – he only had four, increasing to five, of those. He would hold a weekly meeting with his army commanders and would generally have guests to a working dinner each evening before retiring early after a final briefing from the chief of staff. There was, inevitably, a mountain of paperwork to wade through and while some of this would be dealt with by his staff there was also much that could only be actioned by him.

Once Haig assumed the mantle of commander-in-chief he had perforce to deal with a myriad of visitors to his headquarters. Politicians, British and dominion of all hues; Indian princes, foreign potentates, journalists, bishops, industrialists, academics, writers all wanted to hear the General's views and impress him with their own. Increasingly Haig listened and said little, well aware that anything he said could be misconstrued or taken out of context or misquoted, either inadvertently or deliberately. He is accused of being tongue tied, uncommunicative, inarticulate and by extension stupid. That Haig was certainly not stupid is evidenced by the admiration that Haldane – who had a ferocious intellect – had for him, and his work in the War Office, but, while one must beware of national stereotypes, Haig was in many ways the archetypal lowland Scot. He was reserved in manner, and tended to speak only when he had something important to say. He was at ease

58

with those whom he knew well and trusted, but tended to suspect the motives of those whom he did not, particularly if they were politicians. He was by nature somewhat aloof and certainly did not wear his heart on his sleeve, and it is certainly true that while he could speak convincingly on a subject which he had prepared, and his written briefs are clear and unambiguous, he was not good at speaking 'off the cuff'. He would not have been the life and soul of a cocktail party, nor would he have exchanged merry quips and badinage at a dinner party, but amusing cards do not necessarily win battles and one does not have to be a jolly good chap to win wars. That said, Haig did have a sense of humour, albeit usually expressed to his inner circle, and his accession to command was a great relief to his staff and to the wider army. Unlike Sir John French he was not a mercurial personality: he always exhibited a steady, cheerful mien even if inwardly he may have had serious doubts. He worked hard, he was thorough, he avoided sexual indiscretions, he drank moderately, he did not bear grudges and critically he understood that in a coalition war it was essential to maintain good relations with the major ally, his fluent French being immensely helpful. Today it is fashionable to sneer at deeply held religious convictions, but Haig was a product of his upbringing in the Church of Scotland, an austere brand of Protestantism; he often read a chapter of the bible before going to sleep and there can be little doubt that his faith was a great comfort to him in difficult times. All in all he was far more suited to supreme command in the most intensive war that the British had ever or would ever take part in than his predecessor, who lacked the robustness and mental staying power that Haig had in abundance.

Another accusation levelled at Haig is that he was uncaring as to the casualties on the Western Front and that he did not visit the wounded in hospitals. In fact, as a corps and army commander and initially as commander-in chief, he made frequent visits to the wounded, and the effect on him was such that his staff insisted that he stop doing it. There can be no doubt that the sight of one of one's own soldiers lying in a hospital bed suffering from a frightful disfigurement or missing a limb, as a result of orders that one has given, is distressing, and the more there are the more distressing it is, albeit that it is the price that one must pay. There is inevitably a feeling of guilt, however unjustified that may be. Unless one is able to shake that off speedily, it is bound to have an adverse effect on one's performance, as was the case with Haig – or at least so his staff thought – and while he continued to visit the sick and the wounded he did so far less often than hitherto.

As 1916 dawned the war situation showed little hope of an allied victory. It was true that on the Western Front the

Germans had been stopped and were being held, albeit at considerable cost, but the Gallipoli campaign (which Haig had opposed) had been a disaster and troops were being withdrawn. In Mesopotamia the British advance on Baghdad had been halted and apart from the surrender of the German garrison in German South West Africa (now Namibia) little progress had been made in Africa. Haig was now faced with decisions to which he had not been a party, taken at an Allied conference at Chantilly on 6 December 1915 when it had been agreed that all the allies – Britain, France, Russia and Italy – would mount simultaneous attacks on the Germans and Austro Hungarians in 1916. On the Western Front this would involve a combined Anglo French offensive astride the River Somme, coordinated with a Russian drive on the Eastern Front and an Italian advance across the River Isonzo.

The outline plan exposed a fundamental disagreement in principle between Haig and General Joffre. Joffre saw the coming battle as one of attrition, that is a wearing down of the German armies forcing them to throw in their reserves which would also be worn down. That was not the British way of waging war. Mass battles which would develop into crude slogging matches, where the last man left standing was the victor, did not gel with the traditions bequeathed by a small professional army. Haig thought that the offensive should aim to break through the German lines – of which only the first and second were properly constructed – and then exploit through the gap, restoring a war of movement that was more suited to the British way of fighting. In any case the Somme was not an area where vital British interests were at stake: Haig always wanted to launch any major offensive in Flanders, where the security of the Channel Ports was critical and where the Royal Navy was concerned as to the use of German occupied Belgian ports by German submarines, and where there was the possibility of turning the German flank and rolling up their line. It has been said that Joffre chose the Somme as the battleground so as to force the British to take part – it was there that the British sector ended and joined with that of the French – but in fairness to the French the obvious place for a joint operation was where the two joined, otherwise large numbers of troops would have had to be moved many miles to the others' area of operations, with all the administrative and security implications that would be involved. Planning went on apace, and by February 1916 it had been agreed that the British would attack north of the Somme with eleven divisions over a frontage of 14 miles and the French astride and south of the Somme with forty-two divisions over twenty-eight miles. And then on 21 February the Germans attacked at Verdun.

There was no military advantage to holding Verdun, at the point of a salient jutting out into German occupied territory, but the town had a mystical, almost religious, significance for the French. It was there that the heirs of Charlemagne divided the Carolingian empire between them, there that its defenders held out in the Thirty Years War; it became a rallying cry during the French revolution and was the last fortress to fall in the Franco Prussian war of 1870. France would defend Verdun to the last, which is why the Germans launched an attack towards it, intending not to capture it but to entice more and more French troops into the battle until, as the German commander-in-chief put it, the French army would be 'bled white'. At first it seemed that the German plan was succeeding. In April the French contribution to the Somme was reduced to thirty divisions, and in May to twenty-two, and as more and more divisions were sucked into the meat grinder of Verdun there would be but eleven French divisions with two in reserve to take part in the battle which it was now agreed would begin on 1 July. It was now vital that the Somme battle did take place, to take the pressure off the French at Verdun, and whatever Haig and Robertson thought they now had no option but to fall in with Joffre's plans.

The attack would be preceded by an artillery bombardment lasting seven days, with the aim of collapsing the German dugouts and trench systems, cutting the barbed wire in front of them and destroying dumps and forming up places further back. Altogether the British artillery fired almost two million rounds in those seven days. Unfortunately the wire was not cut in all places – shrapnel was inefficient as a wire cutter and high explosive shells only did so if they detonated in contact with the wire, which they usually did not, passing through the wire first. It would not be until the invention of the graze fuse in 1917 that wire could be properly cut by shells. About ten percent of the shells fired were duds, and did not go off at all. At the time it was thought by the conspiracy theorists that this was deliberate sabotage by Irish nationalist factory workers in the United States, where the British had let contracts for much war materiel, but the truth was that both the British and the American armaments industries had to expand enormously and rapidly and the time taken to train munitions workers considerably shortened. Dud shells were due to inexperienced workers, not malicious ones.

At 0730 in the morning of 1 July 1916 around 40,000 British soldiers of the first wave stood up and advanced across no-man's-land towards the German trenches. At first the British field artillery kept firing on the German front line and the attackers could advance unmolested, but as they got closer to their objective the artillery had perforce to switch to shooting at targets farther back, to avoid hitting their own men. Now it was a race: could the attacking infantry get to the opposing trenches before the defenders could get their machine guns up from their dugouts? It was a race that in many areas the Germans won. The artillery had not collapsed the defences as had been hoped, and in the north of the British line the slaughter was appalling, with battalions of 600 men reduced to 200, and little or no ground gained. In the south the picture was much better with all objectives taken and the most southerly battalion advancing seven hundred yards, capturing a major German strongpoint and having only two men killed. In the south the artillery could see what they were hitting, and were helped by the French to their right, which could not be the case in the north. At the end of the first day of the 400,000 British soldiers of the Fourth Army there were sixty thousand casualties, and nineteen thousand of them were dead. It was the largest single day's bloodletting in British military history, and it is all blamed on Sir Douglas Haig.

Men were told that this would be but a stroll in the park – actually they were not told that by anybody in authority nor by anybody with any experience, but they were told to walk steadily, not run. The facts were that it was no good just capturing a line of enemy trench – it had to be held against the inevitable counter attack, and so men had to take with them sufficient ammunition to do that, digging implements to turn the trench round to face the opposite way, grenades, rations and water to see them through the day and their share of sandbags, defence stores and anything else that was considered vital on reaching the enemy line. On average the soldier carried between forty and fifty pounds weight including his boots and his weapon. Not much had changed from Roman times, and a similar load is carried today, although the items may be different and better distributed. Running with such a load was not a sensible option, as the man would arrive at the other end exhausted and in no shape to fight. In any case, this was now an army of Territorials and, in their first major deployment, New Army men, excellent material in many ways but undertrained, inexperienced and led at company and platoon level by, in the main, similarly inexperienced officers. They were simply not capable of anything but the simplest tactics, to attempt anything more sophisticated, as the old regulars could do, would have led to loss of control and chaos. In the French sector the casualties, although serious, were much less. France had pre-war compulsory military service for all males; there was inherent military experience in the civilian population and when the reserves were called up the learning curve was far less steep and far shorter than for the British, who in creating a mass army had to start from scratch.

Despite the loss of life it was more important than ever that the offensive continued, to take the pressure off the French at Verdun and prevent the Germans moving more divisions south. Had the British been able to move the artillery, rotate the troops and bring up more ammunition in time to capitalise immediately on the successes in the south on the first day then great things might have been achieved, but the BEF was not yet capable of such rapid realignment. This was nobody's fault: for the first time in their history the British were fielding a mass citizen army, of pre-war Territorials and New Army units of wartime volunteers, soon to be joined by conscripts. The Brigade, divisional, corps and army commanders were of course officers of the old regular army, but below that were keen but inexperienced officers and NCOs. They would learn, and learn quickly, but while they were doing so a heavy butcher's bill was inevitable. Frontal attacks were unavoidable: the left flank was in the Channel and the right flank on the Swiss border.

The Somme battles went on until November, eventually drawing in over fifty British and almost as many French divisions, and it cost 95,000 British dead and around a third as many French, although of all the British soldiers engaged seventy-four percent emerged without a scratch. But to measure the success or otherwise of a battle by the number of dead is misleading, horrific though that number may be. 1 July 1916 is remembered as the first day of the Somme, but it was also the 121st day of the Battle of Verdun, by which time the French had suffered a quarter of a million casualties. The Somme offensive pulled in sixty-nine German divisions, most of which would otherwise have been moved south to Verdun, where the result cannot then be in doubt, with the probable loss of the war in the west. As it was the Germans had to abandon that offensive. The Somme pushed the Germans back between five and seven miles over a ten mile front, it recaptured seventy square miles of France and fifty-one French towns and villages – in ruins admittedly, but at least reconstruction could begin. It also killed around 150,000 Germans and General Ludendorff, shortly to be chief of the general staff of the German army, said that his army could not withstand another Somme.

4 - Horses, Technology and Stubbornness

Much criticism of Haig stems from the fact that he was a cavalry officer and is hence thought of as being obsessed by the role of the mounted arm, to be a dyed in the wool product of the Victorian army, opposed to any change and deeply suspicious of and opposed to technology. The criticism goes further and alleges that the whole army was dominated by cavalrymen and that the failures on the Western Front stem directly from that fact. Passing by for the moment the allegation that the Western Front was 'a failure', the truth could not be more different.

As for the supposed influence of cavalry officers, in 1914 the commander-in-chief, Sir John French, was a cavalry officer (via the Royal Navy and the Suffolk Artillery Militia) and of the three corps commanders one (Haig) was of the cavalry, one of the artillery (Grierson), followed by an infantryman (Smith Dorrien), and the third, commander III Corps which arrived in September 1914, was another infantryman. On the seven divisions in 1914 five were commanded by infantry officers, one by an artilleryman and only one (the cavalry division) by a cavalry officer. By 1918 of the five army commanders only one, Gough, was of the cavalry, three were from the infantry and one was a Royal Engineer. Of the eighteen corps commanders one was a cavalryman, commanding the cavalry corps, two were engineers, one was a gunner, two were from the dominions (Currie of the Canadian Corps and Monash commanding the Australians) and the remaining twelve were all of the infantry. Not a lot of cavalry dominance there.

As far as the horse is concerned it has to be emphasised that in the early years of the war the horse was the prime mover, the hauler of guns and wagons and the way in which officers got around the battlefield. Each 18 pounder field gun required six horses to pull it, while even in the infantry the commanding officer, all company commanders and the adjutant had horses, which were the equivalent of the Land Rover or the jeep of today. Even by the end of the war, when motorised vehicles were hugely improved and many more were provided and used, the horse was still ubiquitous. Partly this was because the internal combustion engine was not sufficiently robust, and in any case lacked a cross country capability. While the pneumatic tyre had been invented, it was not reliable and once off the road solid rubber tyres sank into anything but the hardest of ground. Altogether the BEF at its height had around 600,000 horses and mules on the Western Front, and only a small minority were for the cavalry.

As for mounted cavalry, the British had a lot less of it as a proportion of the army than did ally or enemy. British cavalry was also different in that it was effectively mounted infantry, trained to move on horseback but where necessary to fight on foot. To that end, again unlike enemy or ally, British cavalrymen were issued with the same rifle as the infantry, rather than a carbine of last resort. A cavalry brigade, being smaller than its infantry equivalent, and needing to tell off one man in four as a 'horse holder' could only provide the equivalent of an infantry battalion when manning the trenches on their feet, but they took their turn as infantry 'up the line', even if they did not like it very much. Despite being trained to act as infantry, the *raison d'etre* of the cavalry was to exploit a breakthrough. If the German defence lines could be broken and a gap created, only the cavalry had the mobility and the speed to stream through the gap and carry the battle forward. That neither side achieved the breakthrough and that only in the early days of the war and the final phases of 1918 did the cavalry have an opportunity to operate in their primary role, does not mean that they were useless, for there were many occasions when tactical successes were achieved by mounted men, even if the great gallop to Berlin never happened.

Unlike both ally and enemy, who depended on universal military service enforced by conscription in peacetime, the British relied on a professional army, and although conscription was introduced for the first time since the English Civil War (when it failed and was abandoned) in July 1916, regular army traditions prevailed. Starting with King Edward I and coming to a peak with Henry V, the English, and later the British, fought their wars with career soldiers. A professional army is, however, expensive – conditions must be sufficiently attractive to persuade men to join, and once in to keep them in. Hence it will inevitably be small. As soldiers in European armies had no choice but to serve, pay and conditions could be much less generous, with only a cadre of long service NCOs and officers needing more spent on their terms and conditions of service. To compensate for lack of manpower in its regular army the English and then the British relied on technology as a force multiplier: the longbow in the Hundred Years War and the Baker rifle in the Napoleonic wars being prime examples. British officers were brought up to understand that principle, and to suggest that the majority in general and Haig in particular were opposed to technological innovation is to fail to recognise the facts. We have already seen how as a young officer Haig, as soon as he heard of the existence of the Maxim machine gun, made the effort to go and find out all about it, and

72

throughout his service he embraced technology, having first satisfied himself that it worked.

On assuming command of the BEF in December 1915 Haig became aware of a project being pursued by the Admiralty, under the aegis of its Landships Committee. Once the Royal Navy, the largest in the world by a considerable margin, had chased German commerce raiders off the seas and had settled down to implement their traditional weapon – the blockade – the Admiralty had plenty of time to devote to 'blue sky thinking'. If the destroyer could roam the oceans at will dealing out death and destruction, could not a similar vehicle be produced for operations on land? Much of the impetus behind the research came from the fertile brain of Winston Churchill, then First Lord of the Admiralty until the Gallipoli fiasco precipitated his sacking, and while many of Churchill's ideas were not far short of lunacy, this one was beginning to bear fruit. Haig immediately despatched a senior staff officer to England to find out all he could about the development of the landship (the cover story for which was the development of a water carrier, hence 'tank'). Haig then applied pressure to speed up the development, agreeing the specifications with the Landships Committee: the tank was to be armoured to provide protection for its crew, be capable of crossing trenches, breaking through barbed wire obstacles, travelling across any ground (hence the caterpillar tracks), providing intimate fire support to the infantry and travelling at the same speed as the infantry (that is at a swift walking pace). Haig ordered 150 of them, to be ready by 1 June 1916. To be fair to the developers, this was an unrealistic demand, but he was told that they could be ready by mid-August. When Haig suggested to Joffre that the Somme offensive be delayed until then, the old warrior exploded, telling Haig that 'the French army will be finished by then'. The start date of 1 July therefore had to stand, and in any case the delivery date now slipped to mid-September. Haig was told that he could have fifty tanks by that date.

There were those in England, and on Haig's staff, who felt that the tank should not be deployed until the full order of 150 was ready, and until further development to improve its performance and reliability could be completed. There was considerable merit in the argument that such a weapon should not be employed until its use could be decisive, but Haig's view, expressed to Robertson, the CIGS in London, was that while accepting all the caveats, anything that saved lives (and after 1 July an average of 500 British soldiers were being killed every day of the Somme offensive) must be made available now.

Forty nine tanks in crates stencilled 'water tanks, Petrograd' were shipped out to the front. Of those thirty-two got to the forming up points for their first use on 15 September. Of those, fourteen broke down before or shortly after crossing the jump off line for the series of attacks. Of the eighteen that did accompany the infantry across no-man's-land six got into shell holes or ditches and could not get out, five were hit by German artillery and could go no further, three were hit by German artillery and went on fire and two went on fire without any help from the Germans. Only two were still functioning at the end of the day. All that notwithstanding, the principle was proved: tanks could cross trenches, they could breach barbed wire and they could support the infantry: one had got the New Zealand division onto their objective, one had enabled the Canadians to take a particularly well defended factory building and two, supported by infantry, had captured High Wood which had held out for a month against successive infantry attacks. The tank was not a war winning weapon – that would not happen until the next world war – nor was it yet a battle winning weapon, but now that the concept was seen to work, Haig's encouragement would ensure that modification and improvement would follow until in 1918 the Mark V tank would truly dictate the course of a battle. The Germans tried to produce something similar, but their soldiers far preferred to use the few British tanks that fell into their hands, rather than relying on their own ungainly and unreliable equivalents.

Like the tank, it was the Royal Navy that began to develop military aviation – an aircraft, whether fixed wing or a dirigible, could allow ships to see far over the horizon, and the idea was soon taken up by the army, and particularly by the Indian Army, whose operations in rugged terrain with no roads were immensely helped by airborne reconnaissance. A sophisticated system of communicating from ground to air on mobile operations in India, especially on and beyond the frontiers, was developed using a frame with black and white squares. Depending on the arrangement of squares messages could be sent to the aircraft overhead, and the aircraft could convey information to the ground by the rather less sophisticated method of wrapping a written note around a stone and dropping it. Haig, from his tours in India, was well aware of the potential of airpower, and the lesson was brought home when in an inter-divisional exercise on pre-war Salisbury Plain, Haig's division was defeated by Grierson's division due to the latter's use of aircraft.

War is a great accelerant of technology, and from the relatively primitive open single-seater machines that accompanied the BEF to France in August 1914 to the recognisably modern bombers and fighters in 1918, Haig ensured that full use was made of the capabilities of the Royal Flying Corps (which embraced army and Royal Naval Air

Service men and machines), whether it was simple reconnaissance and air photography in the early days, to force protection and strategic bombing at the end. There were (and are) many myths surrounding flying during the First World War. It is true that in the early days of military flying there were no dual-seater aircraft: a trainee pilot was given some instruction on the ground, read the manual and then got in and took off. It is true that some pilots arrived at the front having had but a few hours flying experience, but it is not true that the average life of a pilot was six weeks – for a short time the attrition rate of pilots was very high, but extended training and better aircraft soon reduced that. It is true that there were many crashes in the early days, but as the speed was not great and as the aircraft were manufactured from wood and linen, pilots very often walked away from their downed craft. It is also true that parachutes were not provided, not because this would encourage pilots not to press home an attack or to bail out unnecessarily, but because there simply was not room in the early machines for a parachute. Crews of observation balloons were provided with parachutes.

Haig is accused of blindly continuing to throw men at impregnable defences when it had long been clear that such methods did not work. His critics claim that only stubborn persistence in the face of all the evidence prevented him from closing down the Somme offensive after the failure to take all the objectives on the first day and in view of the horrific death toll. But this was a coalition war, and it was not for one participant to opt out, and in any case the situation at Verdun made it imperative that the battle continued. More serious charges are levelled in regard to the next major British operation, that of the Third Battle of Ypres, known colloquially as Passchendaele, although the capture of that village was only one of the battles of the overall offensive. Here Haig, a field marshal from 1 January 1917, is accused of reckless squandering of the flower of British and Empire manhood in attacks over appalling ground which could not possibly succeed, and of insisting on continuing them when it was obvious to everybody that all they produced was more unnecessary slaughter.

Although Verdun had held in 1916, largely due to the British efforts on the Somme, the French government's confidence in Joffre had evaporated, and he was promoted to Marshal and kicked upstairs to a non-job, his place as commander-in-chief being taken by General Robert Nivelle. Nivelle had enjoyed a meteoric rise up the French hierarchy, from a colonel commanding a regiment in 1914 to general and commander-in-chief in two years. He had done well at Verdun, was articulate, politically aware and, having an English mother, spoke that language well. Politicians, both French and British, found him convincing, even if generals, French and British, did not. Nivelle announced that he had the secret, and that he could break through the German lines in forty-eight hours, restoring movement to the front. His plan was for a French offensive in Artois with the British making a subsidiary attack in the Arras area. Once Nivelle had broken through, the British would attack in Flanders and the Belgians and French along the Belgian coast, liberating Ostend and driving into Germany and ending the war. It was a hugely ambitious plan, and it did not work.

The British subsidiary attack did work, when the Canadian Corps captured Vimy Ridge on 9 April 1917. Nivelle's offensive went in on 16 April and while some initial successes were achieved, the advance soon bogged down and the great breakthrough never happened. In May, after a quarter of a million French casualties, Nivelle was asked to resign, refused, blaming his subsidiary commanders for the lack of results, then changed his mind and did resign to be rusticated to French North Africa for the rest of the war, being replaced by Pétain. For the French soldiery it was all too much. Not only had the promises to end the war not been fulfilled, but the generals were falling out amongst themselves all seeking to blame someone else. Widespread mutiny, that most serious of military offences, broke out all over the French army, but while disappointment with the failed campaign was undoubtedly a factor, the immediate causes were those common catalysts of mutiny: conditions of service. The French army was an army of conscripts, where pay was derisory, rations bad and welfare almost non-existent. French soldiers were entitled to a week's leave every four months, but they hardly ever got it, either because of 'the exigencies of the service' – being needed elsewhere – or because the French staff were incapable of making the necessary arrangements. The French never admitted to mutiny, rather the refusals to go into the line, sabotage of transport, singing of the *internationale*, disobedience to orders, attacks on officers and waving of red flags, all encouraged by communists back at home, was described as incidences of 'collective indiscipline'. By July two thirds of the French army on the Western Front was affected, and only draconian security prevented the Germans from finding out. Even the French cabinet were not told the full story, the British cabinet were told virtually nothing and even Haig was not completely aware until he was briefed by Pétain's emissary, when it was made very clear that a major British offensive was essential while Pétain restored the French army to its allegiance – his first step being to send half of the army on leave. The view previously expressed by some French generals that they should do nothing and simply wait for the

Americans, who had declared war in April, was now a non-starter, even if it ever had been otherwise.

Haig, supported by Robertson back at home, had always considered that Flanders was where the main British effort ought to be, and plans had been drawn up for some time. The immediate aim would be to get out of the waterlogged Ypres Salient, surrounded as it was by high ground occupied by the Germans. Before any move out of the Salient could begin, however, Messines Ridge, to the south of the Salient but dominating a large part of it would have to be taken. That task was delegated to the Second Army, commanded by General Sir Herbert Plumer. The attack was preceded by a seventeen day artillery bombardment, when three and a half million shells were fired in the last seven days, compared with two million on the Somme over a much wider front, and on 7 June, preceded by the detonation of nineteen mines each of between 40,000 and 90,000 tons of explosive beneath the German positions, the attack went in. Supported by seventy-four tanks the British (and Australian, and New Zealand) infantry scored a resounding success and by last light on that day they had advanced three miles on a five mile front. The Somme offensive was carried out by an inexperienced and undertrained citizen army, capable of only the simplest of tactical manoeuvres, but the army had learned from the Somme. Now the infantry were using fire and movement, where one sub unit brought down fire on the enemy trenches while another subunit moved forward, to give covering fire in turn. The tanks were Mark IV, far more reliable and efficient than the early examples used on the Somme, and the infantry had trained with the tanks, so that methods of cooperating to take objectives could be worked out. Haig was the driving force behind this transformation: it had been he who insisted that after action reports were prepared and circulated, that lessons were identified and learned, and that training schools were set up to train the troops in the new methods of all arms cooperation. With the taking of Messines, now was the time to burst out of the Salient, but the BEF still did not have sufficient artillery and heavy equipment to mount two major operations simultaneously. The guns would have to be shifted, the ammunition dumps established and the troops brought into position. There would inevitably be a delay, but it was made much worse by political interference.

At home David Lloyd George, a clever and dubious politician, was now Prime Minister. He distrusted soldiers and was not convinced that the BEF should embark on a major offensive at all, particularly as there was to be no French support. With the drowning of Lord Kitchener on his way to Russia in 1916, the CIGS, Robertson, was constitutionally the military adviser to the cabinet and he, briefed by Haig, told the

Prime Minister in his blunt way that the offensive must happen and it must happen as soon as possible. It was only when Lloyd George sought alternative military advice, from Sir John French and Henry Wilson, no fans of Haig, who told him the same thing that in late July he reluctantly agreed that the plan could proceed. To be fair to Lloyd George (which is more than he ever was to anyone) he was not aware of the full situation in the French army, and those few who did know did not tell him as he was notoriously loose tongued.

The third Battle of Ypres started in mist and rain on 31 July when the men of General Sir Hubert Gough's Fifth Army launched a series of hammer blows out of the Ypres Salient. At first all went well and considerable progress was made, and then the weather worsened in the wettest summer for seventy-five years. Movement became difficult, particularly for the artillery and the momentum of the attacks slowed. In late August when it looked as if the rain had eased up Haig ordered a pause to allow the ground to dry out and the troops to recover. On 20 September the battle began again, this time under Plumer. Gough's thrust and aggression was the right spirit to open the battle, now it was Plumer's painstaking and careful planning that was needed. Again, to begin with all went well and 4 October 1917 was described by Ludendorff, chief of staff of the German army, as 'a black day for the German army' when his much vaunted counter attack divisions received a particularly bloody nose at the hands of the BEF. Then the weather turned. Continuous driving rain falling on a drainage system already mostly destroyed by two and a half years of shelling, turned the whole area into a sea of mud. Horses sank hock deep into the mud, the tanks could not operate and the artillery could not get forward. In any other circumstances Haig would have closed the battle down then, even if the final objective, Passchendaele Ridge, had not yet been taken, but the French still needed more time to reconstitute their army, and the battle had to go one. On 7 November, in dreadful conditions, Passchendaele was finally taken, and Pétain was able to inform Haig that his army was ready to resume its role. Pay and rations had been hugely improved, the ringleaders identified and tried (around thirty were executed), and while the mutinies had been resolved, French morale remained brittle for the rest of the war.

The Third Battle of Ypres cost a quarter of a million British and Empire casualties, around 53,000 of them killed. But it had killed a lot more Germans, and it had pulled in eighty-eight German divisions, over half of those they had on the Western Front, and it had dealt them a series of severe blows. It had moved the British positions forward to a far more comfortable and more easily administered line, and now it was the British who held the high ground and who overlooked the Germans, but most of all it had ensured that for the entire period of the battle there was no movement on the French front, and it had bought time for the French army to repair the damage done by the mutinies, time that might otherwise have led to a German victory on the Western Front. The third Battle of Ypres was a bloody battle, but it had to happen, and Haig had no option but to conduct it in the way that he did, and to keep on hammering, regardless of cost.

5 - Haig's Victory

Soldiers, when faced with a problem, consider all the factors, come to a decision as to the best course of action, brief their subordinates accordingly and get on with the matter in hand. Politicians rarely arrive at the best solution: rather they settle with a compromise which everyone can live with, even if it is far from ideal. The mind-set of the soldier is therefore very different from that of the politician, and as long as each keeps to his own sphere that may not matter overmuch. Soldiers in a democracy accepted and accept that it is for the politicians to tell them what to do, but they would prefer not to be told how to do it – rather the armchair strategists should defer to those who have spent their lives preparing and training for war, rather than trying to impose some half-baked flight of fancy onto a situation that they do not understand.

Throughout his tenure as commander-in-chief of the BEF Haig not only had to fight the Germans, he had to contend with his own politicians too, and this became more difficult once Kitchener was no longer Secretary of State for War, and once Lloyd George replaced Asquith as Prime Minister. Lloyd

George and Haig were never going to be compatible personalities: the former was an accomplished orator, a womaniser, deceitful, dishonest, hugely astute, corrupt and often carried away by his own rhetoric, while Haig was taciturn, upright, priggish to an extent and concerned with duty rather than personal advantage. Again, this might not have mattered had not Lloyd George come to convince himself that the Western Front should not be the main theatre of the war, that it was in any case incompetently directed and that Haig should be removed if at all possible. And as Robertson, in his blunt way, constantly poured cold water on Lloyd George's impractical suggestions, then he too should go.

The politicians were divided into two camps – the 'Easterners' and the 'Westerners'. The 'Easterners', led by Lloyd George and Churchill, believed that the war could be won elsewhere than on the Western Front, while the 'Westerners' group of the more sober members of government realised that the Western Front was where the main enemy was, and it was there and only there that he could be defeated. The Lloyd George faction claimed that if the props were knocked away then Germany herself would fall. By the props they meant Austria-Hungary, Turkey and Bulgaria, failing to understand that Germany was the prop, for it was German money, German weapons and German instructors that kept the others in the war.

While Kitchener and then Robertson managed to prevent most of the more ridiculous schemes of the politicians, they could not prevent the Gallipoli shambles, nor the sending of half a million allied troops to Salonika, who sat around doing little other than increasing the rate of venereal disease amongst the French contingent, nor the diversion of seventy six-inch howitzers to the Italians in the Spring of 1917, instead of sending them to Haig for Third Ypres.

When the BEF attacked at Cambrai with nineteen divisions supported by 378 tanks on 20 November 1917, the battle achieved less than it should have done because there were no reserves to capitalise on the initial success. Partly this was because the Battle of Third Ypres had only just finished, but also because Lloyd George had insisted on taking five divisions from the Western Front to send to Italy, to avoid an Italian collapse after the disaster of Caporetto. In fact, the use of those five divisions by Haig would have contributed far more to the ending of the war than avoiding an Italian collapse, for even if Italy was forced out of the war the terrain was such as to prevent any question of the Germans opening up another front from which to attack France, and the Austro-Hungarians were by then in no state to divert troops to the Western, or any other, Front.

Lloyd George very much wanted to replace Haig; his problem was that there was no one else in whom there was so much faith, both in the army and with the public. The only senior general who was sounded out, Plumer, made it very clear that he would not accept the appointment, and the suggestion that the prime minister seriously contemplated putting Monash, the commander of the Australian Corps, in command is risible. Lloyd George's conviction that the casualties in the BEF were unnecessary and that Haig and the generals were profligate with their men's lives, led him to prevent infantry reinforcements who were sitting in England doing nothing being sent out to join the BEF in the face of intelligence that predicted a major German offensive in the spring of 1918 – an assessment that Lloyd George did not accept but which happened as predicted. When challenged in the House of Commons as to his keeping of the reinforcements at home, he stated that the strength of the army in January 1918 was 'considerably greater' than it had been in January 1917. On the face of it Lloyd George was right: the ration strength of the BEF was indeed over 200,000 men greater in 1918, but over 300,000 men of the BEF were not soldiers at all, but in the Labour Corps, which had not existed the previous year and which was made up of labourers from South Africa, China and India whose role was to provide unskilled labour for road making, barrack building, drainage digging, loading and unloading of vehicles and the like. Stout fellows all, none were the equivalent of a soldier with a rifle and bayonet. Lloyd George knew this very well, and when Major General Maurice, in the War Office, wrote a letter to the newspapers exposing the prime minister's duplicity, Maurice was sacked. With the prime minister refusing to allow reinforcements for France, and at the same time agreeing with his French opposite number, Georges Clemenceau, that the BEF would take on more and more sectors of front, Haig had no option but to reduce brigades from four battalions to three, meaning that a division would now be reduced from twelve battalions to nine, but still covering the same, or in some cases a greater, length of front. No commander in the field should ever have been subject to the political interference and lack of support as was Haig by his own prime minister.

To Hindenburg and Ludendorff, now not only commanding the German army but effectively the state as well, the situation at the end of 1917 was dire. Unrestricted submarine warfare had failed to knock the British out of the war and had brought the Americans in; a combination of the Royal Navy, sequestered German ships confined to American ports since the outbreak of war and the US merchant marine had transported a million men of the US army to France, with more to come; the ending of the war on the Eastern Front had not allowed the transfer of as many German divisions as had been hoped, largely due to the need to police the vast swathes of eastern territory annexed by Germany; the Battle of Third Ypres had savaged the German army in the west; and at home the Royal Naval blockade had reduced the civilian population to a state not far from starvation. There was only one chance left of winning the war, and that was by defeating the French and British before the Americans could make themselves felt. By concentrating all their assets and striking at the join between the British and the French, while forcing them to shift their reserves away from the area of main effort, a wedge could be driven between the two, forcing the French to fall back to defend Paris and the British to the Channel ports. It was a huge gamble and if it failed there would be nothing else; Germany's last throw would either win the war in the spring of 1918 or make eventual defeat inevitable.

The last throw, the *Kaiserschlacht*, did not work. Initially a series of hammer blows drove the allied line back. It was a close run thing, and at one point Haig issued a 'backs to the wall' order, but while the line stretched and stretched it never broke, and when eventually the German thrust ran out of momentum they had shot their bolt and there was not another to shoot. German vehicles were running on metal because the blockade prevented the import of rubber for tyres; despite priority for foodstuffs going to the army, the contents of over-run British ration dumps contrasted sharply with the German black bread, sausage and ersatz coffee; morale began to crack, and, almost unbelievably, there were instances of German soldiers refusing the orders of their officers. Now all the Germans could do was to remain on the defensive, in positions that were still very strong, and hope that exhaustion would force the allies to the conference table.

It was not to be. After more political wrangling and the appointment of Marshal Ferdinand Foch as coordinator of allied efforts, a persuader and not, it must be stressed, an overall commander-in-chief, it was agreed that there would be a combined offensive by the Belgian, British, French and American armies with the aim of knocking the Germans off their defensive positions, driving them back into Germany and bringing the war to an end. In the meantime the lessons of the *Kaiserschlacht* were absorbed, training went on apace with the emphasis on breaking through trench lines and then reverting to manoeuvre warfare, with infantry platoons reorganised to reflect what was hoped to be the next phase of the war, and particular attention was paid to all arms co-operation.

For the BEF the great advance began on 8 August 1918 in what would be named the Battle of Amiens. This was a very different army to that which had gone over the top at the

Somme two years before, or even the one that had attacked at Ypres the previous year. In July 1916 the BEF was an army of Territorials and patriotic wartime volunteers, leavened with sprinkling of regulars but undertrained and inexperienced, yet learning quickly. By 1917 it was far more competent yet still short of artillery. Now it was a thoroughly professional force, honed by experience and well led at the junior level by men who had learned their trade the hard way, by surviving, and with all the guns it wanted, plenty of tanks and a mass of aircraft of all types. Surprise was complete, and with the infantry, the armour, the artillery, the engineers and the air all working together to produce shock on the battlefield, this was the birth of what would be called *blitzkrieg* in the next war. Supported by 552 tanks and with the engineers well forward to deal with obstacles, strong points were bypassed to be dealt with by follow-on troops, and by last light the BEF had advanced eight miles. It was the beginning of the Hundred Days, when the Germans were driven back with no opportunity to regroup, the famed Hindenburg Line was breached and they were pushed back almost to where they had started. At last, with defeat on the battlefield and near revolution at home, the Germans sued for peace. The Hundred Days was very much a British led campaign; true, the French too made considerable advances but they were still weary and cautious after the mutinies, and the

Americans, through no fault of their own, were too new to modern warfare to show their undoubted potential.

On 11 November 1918 the war came to an end, and it was Haig's victory. It was he who had expanded and trained and deployed and fought the BEF until it was the only army capable of defeating the Germans on the field of battle – and whatever the propagators of the 'stabbed in the back' myth might say later, the German army was roundly defeated militarily.

At home Haig was feted as the hero of the hour by press and public. He refused to accept any honours until the government did something for the wounded and maimed of the war, which eventually, and reluctantly, they did. He was appointed as commander-in-chief Home Forces, but when that command was abolished in 1920, he was not offered another job. He could justifiably have expected to become CIGS, or to have been offered a governor-generalship, or even to have been made Viceroy of India, but the mean spirited Lloyd George, still smarting at his inability to remove the man he blamed for not winning the war far earlier and at far less cost, would not budge: now was payback time and the prime minister revelled in it. Haig spent the rest of his life working for the welfare of ex-servicemen. He persuaded the plethora of often quarrelling veterans' organisations to come together, as they did in the British Legion, an organisation which Haig did not found but who's patron he became. He lobbied industrialists, employers and trade union leaders in his efforts to find employment for discharged soldiers, sailors and airmen, particularly the disabled. He was tireless in promoting the welfare of men who had served and who had fallen on hard times, and he insisted in answering all the many appeals for help from individuals by a personal handwritten letter.

***

On Sunday 29 January 1928 Field Marshal Earl Haig died of a massive heart attack at his sister's flat in London. He was only sixty-six, worn out by the strains of the war and his unflagging efforts for his old soldiers. His coffin lay in Saint Columba's Presbyterian church in Knightsbridge, where twenty-five thousand people filed past each day, and then lay in state in Saint Giles' Cathedral in Edinburgh, where the queues to pass the coffin stretched for over a mile in driving sleet – and these of men and women who had taken an unpaid day off work to pay their last respects to the man who had commanded them or theirs in war and worked for them in peace.

Once Haig was safely dead the destruction of his memory began. In 1933 Lloyd George published the first of his multi volume *Memoirs*, an acerbic, brilliantly written exercise in self-justification and the settling of old scores. In it he traduces Haig and the generals and shifts all blame for the disasters and the casualties on to them and away from the politicians. As Lloyd George was the Prime Minister for the last three years of the war, and in the cabinet for almost all of it, he cannot escape much of the blame – if blame there is – himself, but instead he remarked on publication that he was sorry that Haig and Robertson were no longer alive to see him blow their reputations away. Churchill, no doubt still rankling at being blamed (rightly) for Gallipoli, damned Haig with faint (very faint) praise. Sir John French's son published a fulminatory attack on Haig, blaming him for his father's removal. The so called 'war poets', no doubt realising that paeans to 'decent men doing their best in a war the nature of which no one had expected' would be unlikely to sell, concentrated instead on the horrors of the trenches and the unnecessary sacrifice of it all. As a generation grew up that had not fought in the war and that was increasingly anti-war, they asked why did it happen and assumed that all those men who died need not have done, and as somebody had to be to blame, it must have been the generals who commanded them, and particularly the man at the top, Haig. Field Marshal Montgomery, a man of far less ability than Haig and faced with problems of much lesser magnitude as he commanded an army a quarter of the size, polished his own image by lauding himself and denigrating Haig. Probably the greatest post Second World War influence on the perception of

Haig has been Joan Littlewood's 1969 play, later turned into a film at the height of the Cold War, 'Oh! What a Lovely War', the adviser to which, the Labour MP Raymond Fletcher, was later exposed as a Soviet agent. Later, the brilliant and hugely popular 'Blackadder Goes Forth', wonderful to watch but about as true to historical facts as 'Winnie The Pooh' portrayed Haig as stupid, hidebound and uncaring, an image that characterises the view of many today.

***

Douglas Haig was shy, reserved, uncomfortable in speaking ex tempore, and uninterested in public relations. He distrusted journalists, even those who, like Repington, were his supporters, and he was suspicious of politicians. He never played to the gallery and did not wear his heart on his sleeve. His religious faith was deeply felt and low church, and he harboured an unreasonable animosity towards Roman Catholicism. He was independently wealthy, wealth that he had not earned, which for some inexplicable reason is sometimes held against him. We might now argue that he was too inclined to accept the views of subordinates that he trusted, and that there were occasions when he could and should have overruled some of the army commanders, but that was not the way things were done then, and his experiences in the Sudan war made him reluctant to interfere. He disapproved of those whose behaviour was, in his eyes, ungentlemanly, he drank only in moderation and was not a hearty, amusing, clubbable companion. His driving forces were duty, loyalty to the King and to the army, and apart from country pursuits – hunting, fishing, polo – he was interested in little else. These personality traits might not have made him the man one would want to sit next to at a dinner party, but neither do they make him unsuitable to command Britain's armies in the most intense war she had ever or has ever fought.

All of Haig's military career leading up to the First World War was to prepare him for the supreme command: top at Sandhurst, highly thought of at Staff College, proficient as a staff officer and a sound and courageous leader of men, both of his own race and of others. Contact with and an understanding of the armies of the Empire, and his acceptance of the unarguable fact that on land Britain's armies would always operate as part of a coalition, and that an ability to get on with allied officers and to understand the parameters within they had to work was an essential part of being a successful British commander, were all part of Haig's development. He was highly intelligent and never averse to new – even revolutionary – ideas as demonstrated by his work with Haldane in devising and implementing the most drastic and arguably the most important reforms the British army has ever been subject to.

As a corps and then army commander in 1914 and 1915 he did little wrong: he was forced to close the Battle of Neuve Chappelle because there was insufficient artillery ammunition to carry on, and at Loos he was surely right when he asked for the reserves to be much closer to the front and available much earlier than they were. By the end of 1915 when it was increasingly obvious that Sir John French was incapable of commanding the ever expanding forces that the British were putting in the field, Haig was the obvious man to replace him, and that was the opinion of the king, the Secretary for War and, importantly, the BEF in France.

As the junior partner in the alliance the British had no option but to go along with Joffre's plan for the Somme offensive in 1916, and once the Germans attacked at Verdun and the British were now to play the major part, that offensive had to happen when it did and it had to continue to keep the pressure away from the French. In the end, despite the death toll, the Somme did more damage to the Germans than it did to the British. Third Ypres forced the Germans to wager everything on the last throw of the Kaiser's Offensive in 1918, and it was that that lost them the war. Far from being the hidebound technophobe of popular legend, Haig embraced technology – tanks, gas, flamethrowers, aircraft, radio – and anything that could substitute for manpower and hence reduce casualties.

Certainly the casualties of the war were horrific, far more than Britain had suffered in any war before or since, but considerably less in proportion than ally or enemy. None of the many critics of Haig have ever said how they would have conducted the war, nor how all those casualties might have been avoided. Wars cannot be fought without casualties, and as there was no alternative to frontal attacks by infantry until very late in the war, then a high death rate was inevitable, particularly so when those attacks were perforce carried out by 'pals' battalions with little experience and minimal training. Any idea of holding back until Britain had a large and well trained and equipped army and then intervening to win the war and deciding the shape of Europe was simply not possible – it would have been unacceptable to the French and in any case would probably have caused them to lose the war before the mass British army could make itself felt.

This was a necessary war in which for very good moral and practical reasons Britain had to take part. No amount of secondary theatres or politicians wheezes could avoid the fact that it was on the Western Front and only on the Western Front that Germany could be defeated. Side shows such as Gallipoli and Salonika, that politicians insisted on, or invasions of Schleswig Holstein or landings in Zeebrugge, which politicians suggested but were talked out of, were not going to do it: only hard, vicious and continual battles on the main front, with the concomitant loss of life, could.

Douglas Haig crossed to Europe in August 1914 and stayed there until the war ended in 1918. For most of that period he commanded an army larger than any Britain has ever put in the field and from December 1915 he managed the transition from a relatively tiny force of a few hundred thousand to a citizen army of almost two million. In 1918 it was his army that led the allies to victory. As a commander there were none who could have bettered Haig, and very few who could have equalled him.

In 1918 victory was celebrated and Haig was feted as a hero. It is high time that Haig's reputation was restored and that he is celebrated as a hero now.

Select Bibliography

Beckett, IFW, *The Great War 1914-18,* Longman Harlow, 2001.

Bond, B (Ed) *Look to your Front: Studies in the First World War,* Spellmount Staplehurst, 1999.

Corrigan, Gordon, *Mud, Blood and Poppycock: Britain and the First World War*, Cassell London, 2003.

Corrigan, Gordon, *Loos: The Unwanted Battle*, Endeavour Press, 2015.

Edmonds, JE, *Military Operations France and Belgium* (14 vols) HMSO/MacMillan London 1922 – 1947.

French, Major the hon Gerald, *French Replies to Haig,* Hutchinson London, 1936.

Lloyd George, David, *War Memoirs* (2 vols), Odhams London, 1936, 1938.

Mead, Gary, *The Good Soldier, the* B*iography of Douglas Haig,* Atlantic London, 2007.

Philpott, WJ, *Anglo-French Relations and Strategy on the Western Front 1914 – 1918,* MacMillan London, 1996.

Reid, Walter, *Douglas Haig: Architect of Victory,* Birlinn Edinburgh, 2006.

Scott, Douglas (Ed), *Douglas Haig – Diaries and Letters 1861-1914,* Pen & Sword Barnsley, 2006.

Sheffield, Gary, *The Chief: Douglas Haig and the British Army,* Aurum London, 2011.

Sheffield, Gary & Bourne, J, *Douglas Haig – War Diaries and Letters 1914 – 1918,* Weidenfeld & Nicolson London, 2005.

Terraine, J, *The Western Front 1914-1918,* Hutchinson London, 1964.

Terraine, J, *To Win a War: 1918,* Sidgwick & Jackson London, 1978.

Woodward, DR, *Lloyd George and the Generals,* University of Delaware Press Newark NJ, 1983.

Printed in Great Britain
by Amazon